Guess What

Published in the United States of America by
Cherry Lake Publishing
Ann Arbor, Michigan
www.cherrylakepublishing.com

Content Adviser: Susan Heinrichs Gray
Reading Adviser: Marla Conn, ReadAbility, Inc.
Book Design: Felicia Macheske

Photo Credits: © defpicture/Shutterstock.com, cover; © Stana/Shutterstock.com, 1, 4; © Cosmin Nahaiciuc/Shutterstock.com, 3, 11; tiverylucky/Shutterstock.com, 7; iKhai_TH/Shutterstock.com, 8; © Fernando Cortes/Shutterstock.com, 13; © Michiel de Wit/Shutterstock.com, 14; © Butterfly Hunter/Shutterstock.com, 17; © RoscoPhoto/Thinkstock, 18; © Taiftin/Shutterstock.com, 21; © Eric Isselée/Shutterstock.com, back cover; © Andrey_Kuzmin/Shutterstock.com, back cover

Library of Congress Cataloging-in-Publication Data

Calhoun, Kelly, author.
 Scaly swimmers / Kelly Calhoun.
 pages cm. — (Guess what)
 Summary: "Young children are natural problem solvers and always looking for answers, especially when it involves animals. Guess What: Scaly Swimmers: Crocodile provides young curious readers with striking visual clues and simply written hints. Using the photos and text, readers rely on visual literacy skills, reading, and reasoning as they solve the animal mystery. Clearly written facts give readers a deeper understanding of how the animal lives. Additional text features, including a glossary and an index, help students locate information and learn new words."
— Provided by publisher.
 Audience: Ages 5-8
 Audience: K to grade 3
 Includes index.
 ISBN 978-1-63362-629-4 (hardcover) — ISBN 978-1-63362-719-2 (pbk.) — ISBN 978-1-63362-809-0 (pdf) — ISBN 978-1-63362-899-1 (ebook)
 1. Crocodiles—Juvenile literature. 2. Children's questions and answers. I. Title.

QL666.C925C35 2016
597.98'2—dc23

2015003098

Cherry Lake Publishing would like to acknowledge the work of The Partnership for 21st Century Skills.
Please visit *www.p21.org* for more information.

Printed in the United States of America
Corporate Graphics Inc.

Table of Contents

My feet have sharp claws.

My body is covered with scaly skin.

I have a strong tail that helps me swim.

My ears close to keep out water.

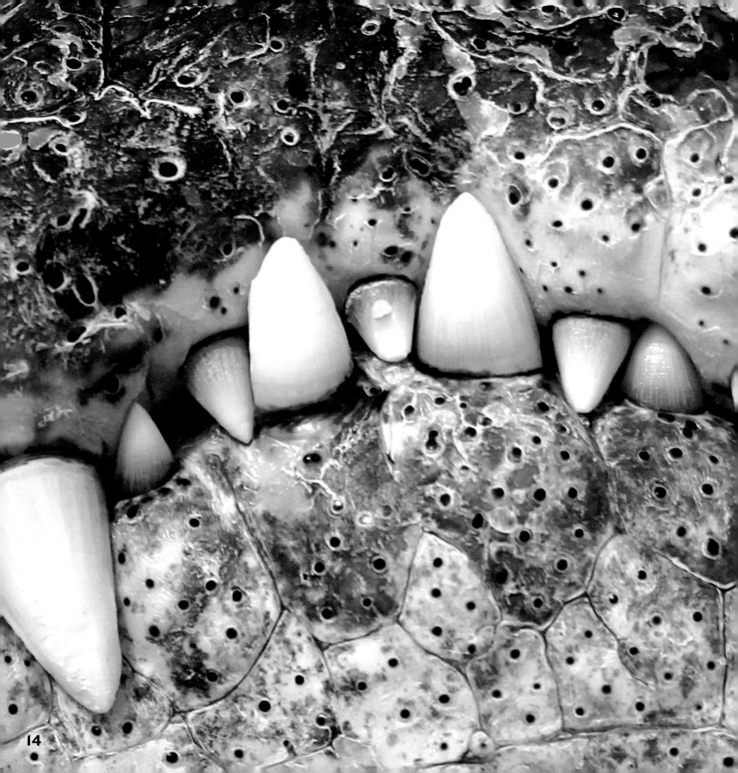

14

I have long rows of teeth.

I have powerful jaws.

CHOMP!

I spend a lot of time in the water.

Do you know what I am?

I'm a Crocodile!

About Crocodiles

1. A crocodile's eyes are on the top of its head.

2. The long, powerful tail of a crocodile helps it swim.

3. Crocodiles use their strong jaws to bite down on **prey**.

4. Crocodiles can go for days without eating.

5. Crocodiles usually eat small **mammals**, birds, fish, crabs, insects, snails, and frogs.

Glossary

jaws (jawz) the bones that frame an animal's mouth

mammals (MAM-uhlz) animals that have hair or fur and usually give birth to live babies

scaly (SKAYL-ee) covered in thin, flat, overlapping pieces of hard skin

sharp (shahrp) having an edge or point that cuts or pierces easily

prey (pray) an animal that is hunted by another animal for food

Index